Fill in the missing regions on the timeline

(choose from America, Oceania and the Middle East)

years BC				years AD			
1500	1000	500	0	500	1000	1500	2000

Africa

....

Asia

Europe

....

....

Answers

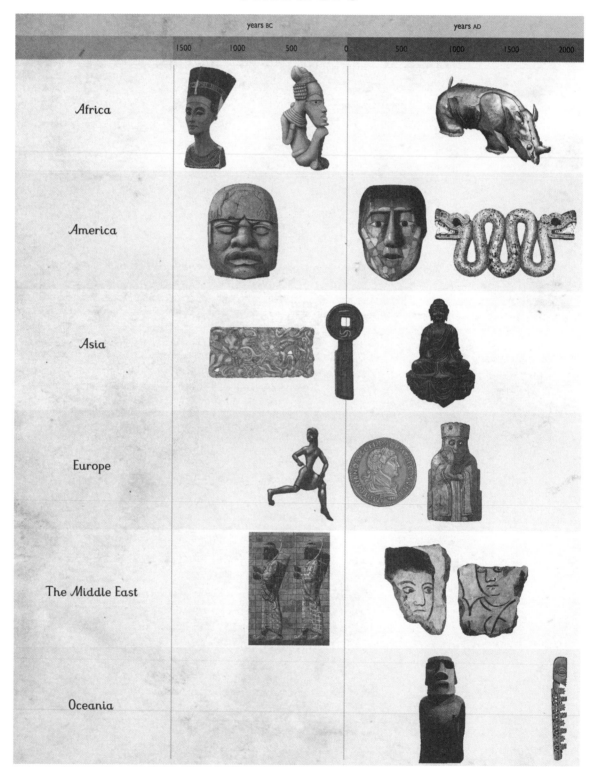

Complete this *Aztec* mosaic of a double-headed serpent

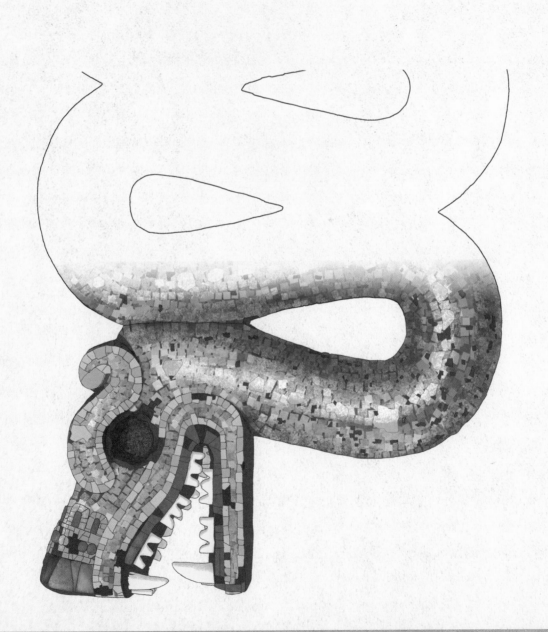

Double-headed serpent mosaic
Fifteenth or sixteenth century AD
America – The Aztecs

Around two thousand tiny pieces of turquoise have been
meticulously arranged on carved wood to form this serpent.

Spot the difference

(there are 10 differences to spot)

Answers

Fresco from Pompeii
First century AD
Europe – Ancient Rome

How to draw the Eye of Horus

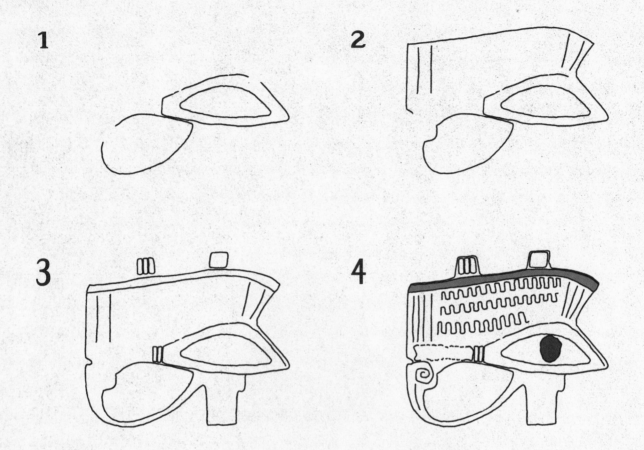

1

2

3

4

Try it yourself

Faïence *wedjat* eye
1069–945 BC
Africa – Ancient Egypt

The *wedjat* eye, also known as the Eye of Horus,
was an Egyptian healing symbol and
a very popular amulet design.

Spot the pairs from the same region

(objects are from Rome, Mesopotamia and Southern Africa)

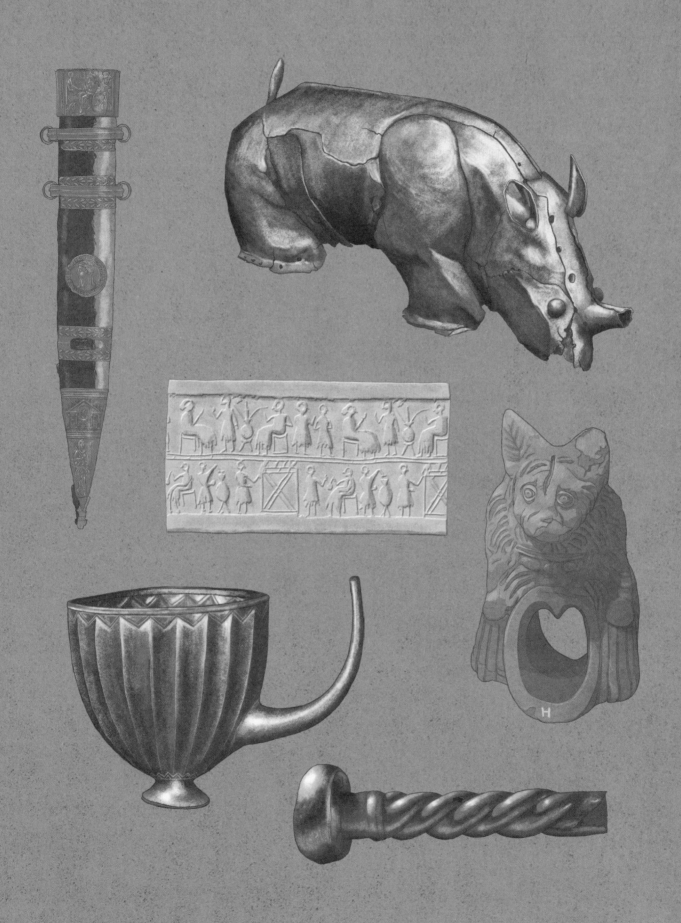

Answers

Europe - Ancient Rome

The sword of Tiberius
First century AD

Water spout
First century AD

The Middle East - Mesopotamia

Royal cemetery, Ur: gold cup
Around 2600–2400 BC

Royal cemetery, Ur: seal
Around 2600 BC

Southern Africa

Mapungubwe rhinoceros
AD 1220–1290

Gold sceptre
AD 1220–1290

Add more *moai* statues to this picture of Easter Island

Hoa Hakananai'a, Rapa Nui
Around AD 1000
Oceania – Polynesia

The people of Rapa Nui, or Easter Island, produced
hundreds of astonishing stone statues, known as *moai*.
Some are up to 10m (33ft) tall.

What can you see in the Standard of Ur?

Can you spot the fish?
Can you spot the musician?
How many figures are holding glasses?

How many goats are there?
Can you spot the lion?
Which figure do you think is the king?

Answers

Royal cemetery, Ur: Standard of Ur
Around 2600–2400 BC
The Middle East – Mesopotamia

This wooden box, inlaid with mosaic, is a work of art
from the Sumerian period. Its purpose is unknown.

Copy this terracotta figure onto the grid

Nok terracotta figure
Sixth century BC–sixth century AD
Western Africa

This terracotta figure is from the Nok culture, which is named after the
village where the first terracotta sculpture of this kind was found.
Other sculptures, including human heads, figures and animals
have been discovered across an area hundreds of square miles wide.

Who do you think owned the following objects?

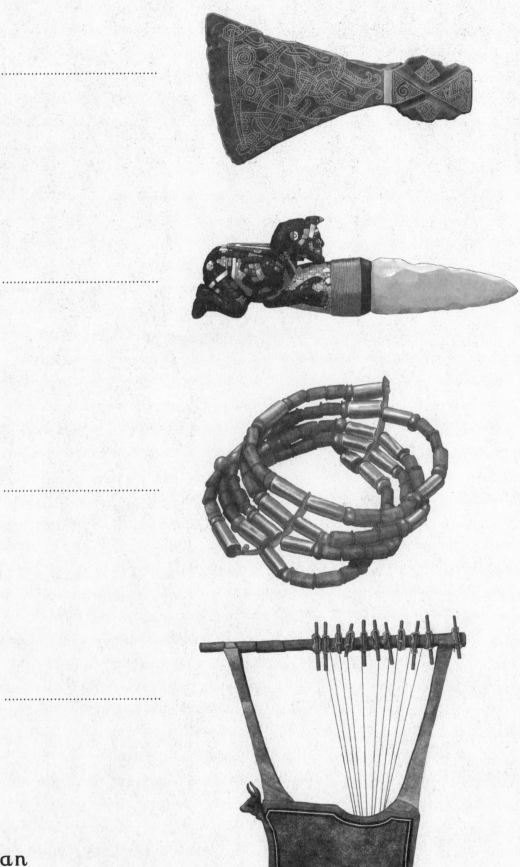

....

....

....

....

Queen
Priest
Musician
Warrior

Answers

Silver-inlaid axehead
– this belonged to a warrior
Tenth century AD
Europe – The Vikings

Mosaic ceremonial knife
– this probably belonged to an Aztec priest
Fifteenth–sixteenth century AD
America – The Aztecs

Royal cemetery, Ur: cuff beads
– these belonged to a female member
of royalty, possibly a queen
2600–2400 BC
The Middle East – Mesopotamia

Royal cemetery, Ur: silver lyre
– this belonged to a musician
2600–2400 BC
The Middle East – Mesopotamia

Create your own story on this Greek vase

Black-figured amphora
Around 530–520 BC
Europe – Ancient Greece

The painting on this wine jar shows a scene from Homer's epic poem, the *Iliad*, where the warrior hero Achilles kills the Amazon queen, Penthesilea.

Find a way through the maze to the face at its centre

Start

Answer

Sun stone
AD 1250–1521
America – The Aztecs

This intricately carved sun stone was once part of a temple complex in Tenochtitlán. It is also known as a calendar stone, because it features the 20 Aztec day names that formed the basis of their sacred calendar.

Circle the coins from Ancient Rome

Answers

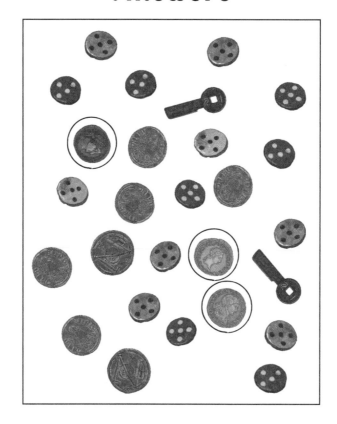

Roman coins
First, second and fourth centuries AD
Europe – Ancient Rome

Vale of York coins
AD 927
Europe – The Vikings

Bronze knife coin
AD 7
Asia – Ancient China

Royal cemetery, Ur: board game pieces
Around 2600–2400 BC
The Middle East – Mesopotamia

Finish the Colossal head

Colossal head, number five
1200–900 BC
America – The Olmec

This is one of 17 colossal stone heads found in Mexico.
The distinctive facial features of each one indicate that they are
unique portraits of real people, probably Olmec rulers.

Finish drawing the patterned tiles on this board game

Royal cemetery, Ur: board game
Around 2600–2400 BC
The Middle East – Mesopotamia

Examples of board games with 20 squares have been found
from the eastern Mediterranean and Egypt across to India
and date from 3000 BC to the first millennium AD.

Number these figurines according to their age

1 being the oldest and 8 the most recent

1. 2500 BC

2. 1900 BC

3. 1500 BC

4. 900-500 BC

5. 100 BC-AD 400

6. 500 AD

7. 1400 AD

8. 1700-1800 AD

Answers

1. Around 2500 BC: **Indus dancing girl,** Asia – Ancient India

2. Around 1900 BC: **Wooden model of bakers,** Africa – Ancient Egypt

3. Around 1500 BC: **Statue of Idrimi,** The Middle East – The Ancient Levant

4. 900–500 BC: **Seated female figurine,** America – The Olmec

5. 100 BC–AD 400: **The Wray Figurine,** America – The Hopewell

6. Around 500 AD: **Kofun tomb figure,** Asia – Ancient Japan

7. Around 1400 AD: **Great Zimbabwe soapstone figure,** Southern Africa

8. 1700–1800 AD: **God figure A'a, Austral Islands,** Oceania – Polynesia

Colour in this page from the Lindisfarne Gospels

Page from the Lindisfarne Gospels
Around AD 700
Europe – The Celts

The Lindisfarne Gospels give stunning examples of the blend between
Celtic culture and Christian worship. This book's illuminated text is
the work of a single artist, possibly a bishop or abbot.

Spot the difference

(there are 10 differences to spot)

Answers

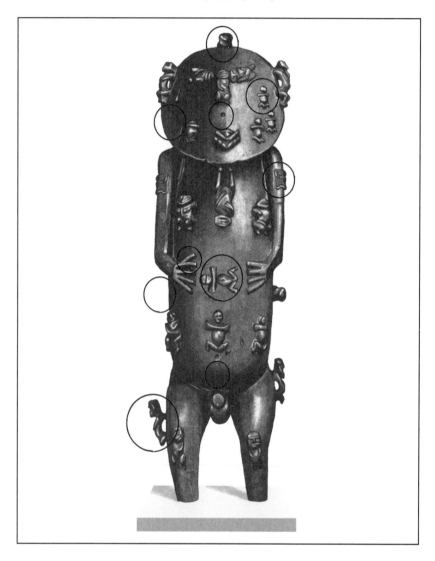

God figure A'a, Austral Islands
Eighteenth–early nineteenth century AD
Oceania – Polynesia

This carving, from the Austral island of Rurutu, is thought to
represent the local deity, A'a, in the act of creating people.

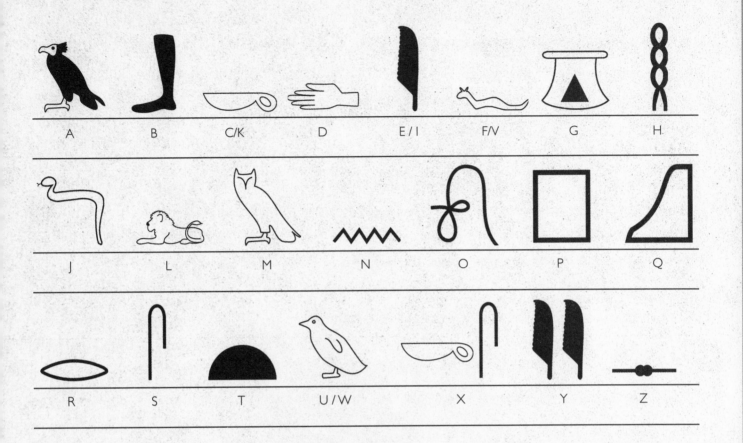

A B C/K D E/I F/V G H

J L M N O P Q

R S T U/W X Y Z

Write your name in hieroglyphs

Page from the Book of the Dead of Hunefer
Around 1300 BC
Africa – Ancient Egypt

The Book of the Dead contained beautifully illustrated instructions on
how to perform a proper burial and achieve a safe passage to the next life.

Draw in the missing bricks in this frieze

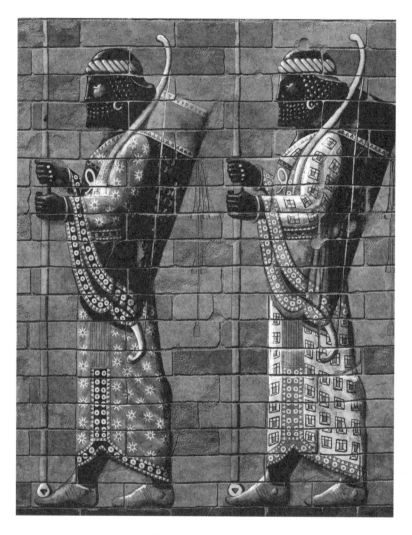

Frieze of Archers
Around 510 BC
The Middle East – Ancient Persia

The colourful glazed bricks that make up this stunning frieze were discovered
during excavations at the site of Darius the Great's palace at Susa.
Thousands more glazed bricks have been discovered at the site, suggesting that
processions of archers may have covered hundreds of metres of the exterior palace walls.

How many animals can you spot in this belt buckle?

Answers

Gold belt buckle
Second century BC
Asia — Ancient China

This buckle is one of over two thousand objects recovered
from a tomb at Shizishan in western China. The expertly executed
image on this buckle is of a tiger and a bear attacking a horse.

Find the missing square

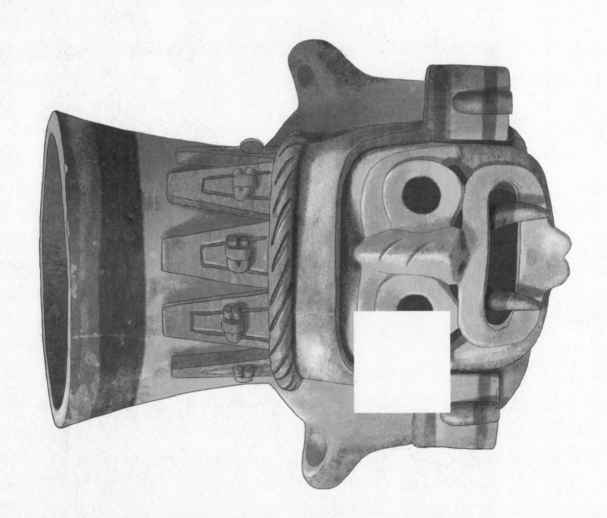

Answers

Pot depicting Tláloc
Fifteenth century AD
America – The Aztecs

Tláloc was the Aztecs' rain god and one of their most important deities.
This pot shows Tláloc painted blue to symbolise water and wearing a pointed
headdress to represent the mountains, a precious source of water.

Draw the mummy mask

Mummy mask

Gilded mummy mask
Late first century BC–early first century AD
Africa – Ancient Egypt

Mummy masks like this one were placed inside Egyptian
coffins over the face and shoulders of the mummy.

Draw a line connecting each item to its proper name

Amphora   Sceptre   Mosaic   Torc   Seal   Amulet

Answers

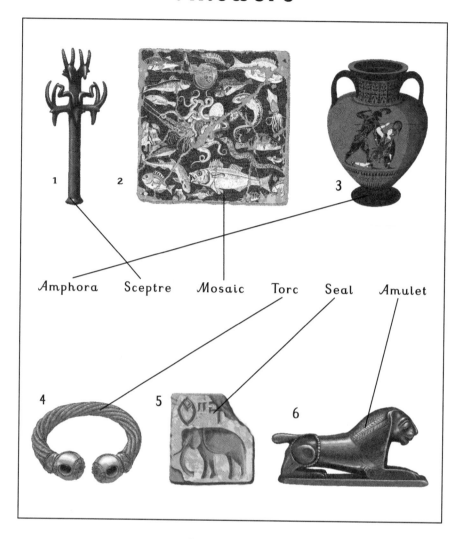

Amphora   Sceptre   Mosaic   Torc   Seal   Amulet

1. Copper sceptre
4500–3500 BC
The Middle East – The Ancient Levant

2. Mosaic
Second century AD
Europe – Ancient Rome

3. Black-figured amphora
Around 530–520 BC
Europe – Ancient Greece

4. The Great Torc of Snettisham
75 BC
Europe – The Celts

5. Carved steatite seal
2600–1900 BC
Asia – Ancient India

6. Gold amulet of a lion
Around 1650–1550 BC
Africa – Ancient Egypt

Draw this gladiator's helmet

1

2

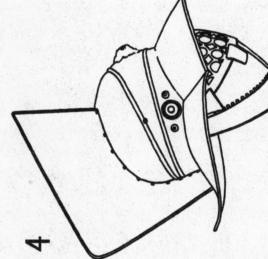

3

4

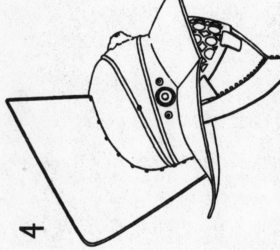

Gladiator's Helmet
First century AD
Europe – Ancient Rome

The gladiators would fight in Roman arenas such as
the Colosseum for the entertainment of the Roman people.
These were usually battles to the death.

Create your own mythical creature based on this sculpture

Lamassu
Around 883–859 BC
The Middle East – Mesopotamia

Standing over 3m (10ft) high and 3m (10ft) long, this imposing
sculpture, known as a *lamassu*, is one of a pair that once stood
as guardians at the palace of Ashurnasirpal II, in the Assyrian
capital, Nimrud. Hybrid mythical creatures, such as this winged,
human-headed bull, were thought to have protective powers.

Label the canopic jars with the organs that were stored inside them

Stomach

Intestines

Lungs

Liver

Answers

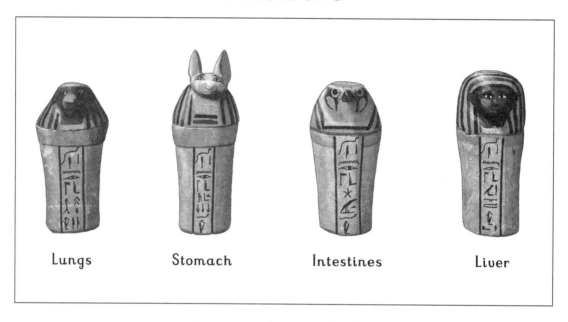

| Lungs | Stomach | Intestines | Liver |

Painted wooden canopic jars
Around 700 BC
Africa – Ancient Egypt

Design another mask in the style of

this jade funerary mask

Jade mosaic funerary mask
AD 683
America – The Maya

This mask, which belonged to Pakal the Great, called
Janaahb' Pakal (Radiant Shield Sun), was discovered in
a royal tomb beneath the Temple of Inscriptions at the
ancient city of Palenque.

Colour in the rest of this Roman mosaic

Mosaic
Second century AD
Europe – Ancient Rome

Wealthy Roman houses were lavishly decorated and floors were often
covered in intricate mosaics. This example shows detailed images of the sort
of Mediterranean seafood that Roman diners would have enjoyed.

Spot the difference

(there are 10 differences to spot)

Answers

Lion-hunting panel
883–859 BC
The Middle East – Mesopotamia

Match these objects to their location of origin on the map

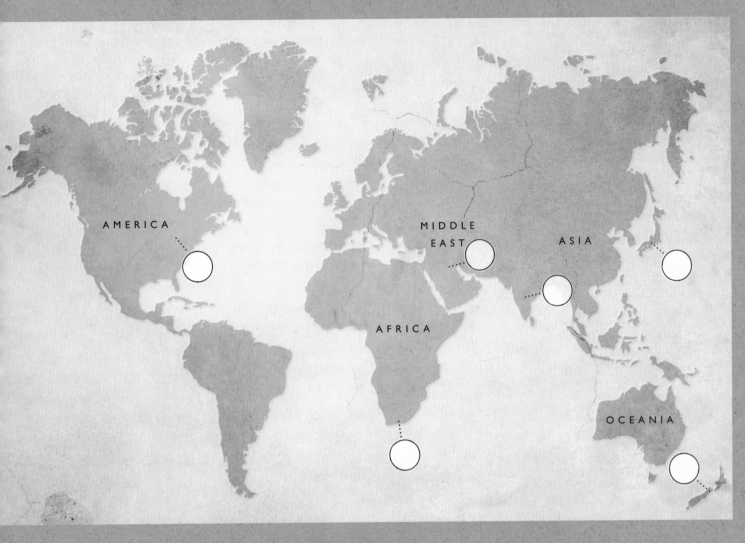

Answers

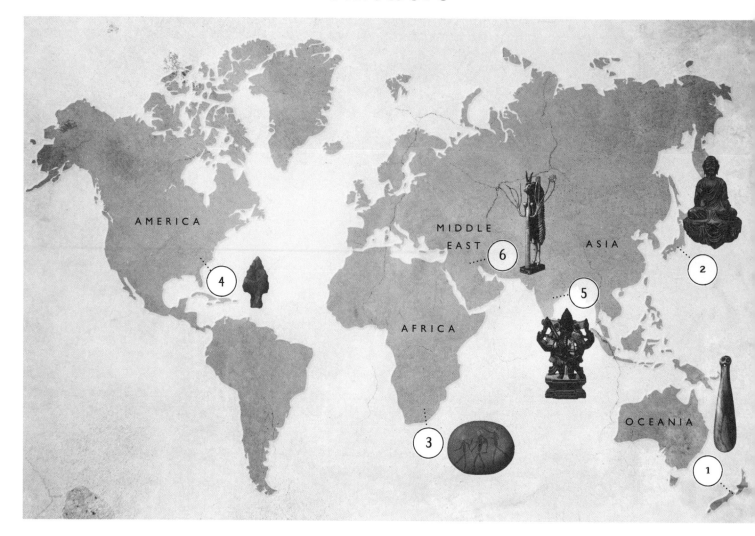

1. Hand club
Late eighteenth–nineteenth century AD
Oceania – The Māori

2. Bronze Buddha
Eighth century AD
Asia – Ancient Japan

3. Coldstream stone
Date unknown
Southern Africa

4. Projectile point
200 BC–AD 500
America – The Hopewell

5. Statue of Ganesha
Eleventh century AD
Asia – Ancient India

6. Royal cemetery, Ur: statuette
Around 2600–2400 BC
The Middle East – Mesopotamia

Add a necklace and earrings to the head of Nefertiti, then colour in her headdress

Bust of Queen Nefertiti
Around 1340 BC
Africa – Ancient Egypt

Nefertiti was the wife of the pharaoh Akhenaten. She was a prominent
queen, ruling alongside her husband and playing an active role.

Colour in this fragment from the Parthenon and draw in the missing faces

Fragment from the Parthenon
Around 438–432 BC
Europe – Ancient Greece

Still visible in modern-day Athens, the Parthenon is the most famous of the ancient buildings in the Acropolis. This fragment is part of a 160m (525ft) long frieze that ran along the outside of the Parthenon. It depicts the procession that took place every year as part of a festival in honour of the goddess Athena.

Add decoration to the Battersea Shield

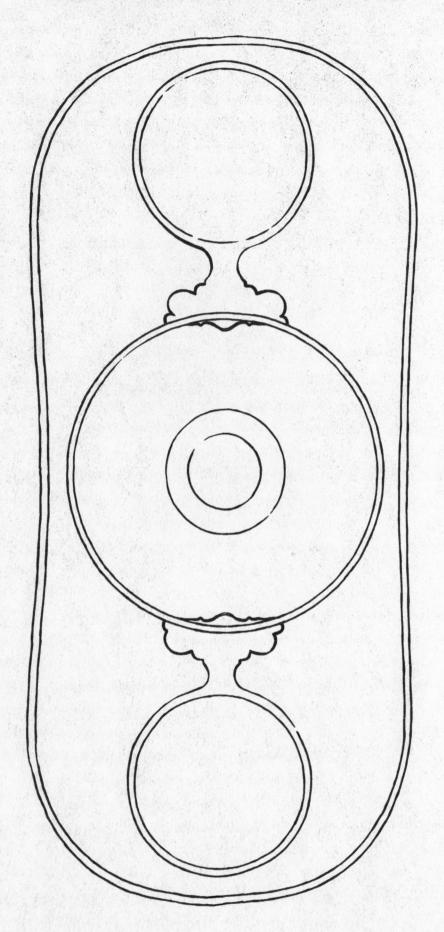

The Battersea Shield
350–50 BC
Europe – The Celts

Warfare was a dominant feature of Celtic life and warriors
were highly respected. With its polished bronze and prominent
red enamel studs, this shield was probably made for display.

Which two objects on this page are not made from clay?

Answers

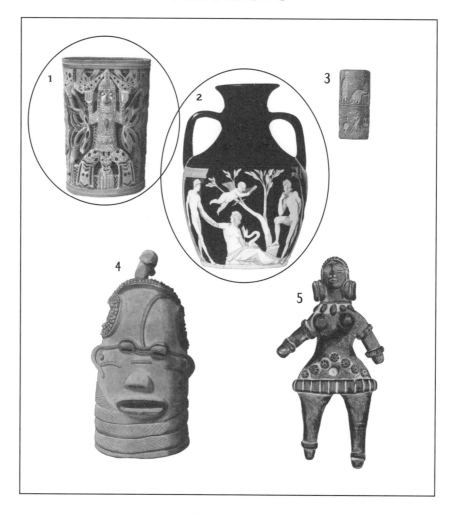

1. Ivory armlet
Fifteenth–sixteenth century AD
Western Africa

2. The Portland Vase, made from cameo-glass
Around AD 5–25
Europe – Ancient Rome

3. Royal cemetery Ur: seal, made from terracotta clay
Around 2600 BC
The Middle East – Mesopotamia

4. Lydenburg head, made from fired earthenware
Around AD 500
Southern Africa

5. Mother Goddess terracotta figurine
Third century BC
Asia – Ancient India

What do you think the rest of this chess set looked like?

Try drawing a knight on a horse, the king
on his throne and a rook, or castle

The Lewis Chessmen
AD 1150–1200
Europe – The Vikings

These chess pieces, carved out of walrus ivory and whales' teeth,
were found in the Isle of Lewis, off the north-west coast of Scotland.

Complete the Egyptian mummy

Gilded outer coffin of Henutmehyt
Around 1250 BC
Africa – Ancient Egypt

Henutmehyt was a priestess from the Egyptian
city of Thebes and it is clear from her lavish burial
that she was extremely wealthy and highly regarded.